D

G

methuen | drama
LONDON • NEW YORK • OXFORD • NEW DELHI • SYDNEY

METHUEN DRAMA
Bloomsbury Publishing Plc
50 Bedford Square, London, WC1B 3DP, UK
1385 Broadway, New York, NY 10018, USA
29 Earlsfort Terrace, Dublin 2, Ireland

BLOOMSBURY, METHUEN DRAMA and the Methuen Drama logo are trademarks of Bloomsbury Publishing Plc

First published in Great Britain 2024

Cover artwork: Tommy Ga-Ken Wan and D8

A catalogue record for this book is available from the British Library.

A catalog record for this book is available from the Library of Congress.

ISBN: PB: 978-1-3505-1590-1
ePDF: 978-1-3505-1591-8
eBook: 978-1-3505-1592-5

Series: Modern Plays

Typeset by Mark Heslington Ltd, Scarborough, North Yorkshire
Printed and bound in Great Britain

To find out more about our authors and books visit www.bloomsbury.com and sign up for our newsletters.

Dear Billy

A Love Letter to the Big Yin

From the People of Scotland

Written and performed by Gary McNair.
Directed by Joe Douglas.

Dear Billy

A Love Letter to the Big Yin
From the People of Scotland

Cast

Musician	Simon Liddell (he/him)
Performer	Gary McNair (he/him)
Musician	Jill O'Sullivan (she/her)

Creative Team

Lighting Designer	Kate Bonney (she/her)
Director/Dramaturg	Joe Douglas (he/him)
Set and Costume Designer	Claire Halleran (she/her)
Lighting Designer	Simon Hayes (he/him)
Composer	Simon Liddell (he/him)
Writer	Gary McNair (he/him)
Director (Remount)	Sally Reid (she/her)
Composer	Jill O'Sullivan (she/her)

Story Gatherer	Robbie Gordon
Story Gatherer (Research)	Jacqueline Houston (she/her)
Story Gatherer	Genevieve Jagger
Story Gatherer	Jamie Marie Leary (she/her)

This show would not be possible without all the people who shared their stories with us.

Dear Billy
A Love Letter to the Big Yin
From the People of Scotland

Was first performed at the Palace Theatre, Kilmarnock on Tuesday 16 May 2023.

Thanks
David Carroll, Lillian Downie, Fiona Johnston, Katy McNair, Brian O'Sullivan, RCS, Dundee Rep, Sally Reid, Gordon Turner, Jamie Gordon, Colin Bell, Will Goulding and Angela Doherty from Connecting Craigmillar from the Thistle Foundation, and all at Craigmillar Hearts Club.

And, of course, the Big Yin.

Kate Bonney (she/her) Lighting Designer

Kate Bonney designs lighting for a wide variety of live performance and events. Her heart lies in creating work that audiences never forget, alongside telling stories that deserve to be told. Recent credits include *Old Boy* with Dundee Rep, *Cyprus Avenue* with the Tron and *Mimi Store* with Jupiter+ on Perth High Street. Kate also forms half of design company Lightworks Events Ltd, alongside Simon Hayes. Together, they led the design of *Enchanted Forest* from 2013 until 2019, designed *My Light Shines On* with Edinburgh International Festival in 2020 during the peak of the pandemic, and last year found themselves designing lighting for a vertical launch space vehicle (a rocket) for a large-scale photoshoot with Orbex, an aerospace company based in Kate's home town of Forres, Moray.

Joe Douglas (he/him) Director/Dramaturg

Joe is a director, writer, creative producer, dramaturg and occasional performer. He is the Chair of Theatre Directors Scotland. He graduated with a BA in Directing from Rose Bruford College, London. For the National Theatre of Scotland, he has directed or co-directed: *Dear Billy*; *The Cheviot, the Stag and the Black, Black Oil*; *Dear Scotland*; *The Last Polar Bears*; *Our Teacher's A Troll*; and *Allotment*. Joe was also Associate Director on three international tours of Black Watch. He was Artistic Director of the Live Theatre in Newcastle upon Tyne (2018–20) and was Associate Artistic Director of Dundee Rep (2016–17). He was Co- Artistic Director (with Gareth Nicholls) of Utter (2011–2017). Joe collaborates regularly with activist and comedian Mark Thomas and has made around fifteen shows at the Òran Mór's A Play, a Pie and a Pint and he will return to direct there in 2024.

Claire Halleran (she/her) Set and Costume Designer

Claire Halleran is a graduate of Glasgow School of Art (BA Hons) and Queen Margaret University (MFA). Claire has designed for numerous theatre companies including the National Theatre of Scotland, Unicorn, Stellar Quines, Grid Iron, Magnetic North, Showroom, Polar Bears, Borderline/Hirtle, Heroica, Cultured Mongrel Dance Theatre, A Moment's Peace, Bubury Banter, Fish and Game, Starcatchers, Visible Fictions, Birds of Paradise, Frozen Charlotte, Platform, RCS and Eco Drama. She has also designed and created interactive events for Edinburgh Science, and film festivals with Tilda Swinton and Mark

Cousins, has been an associate with Punchdrunk Enrichment, and designed both Glasglow and Elfingrove for Itison. She is co-founder of The Envelope Room, a network created in 2013 to support, promote and connect stage designers in Scotland.
www.clairehalleran.weebly.com

Simon Hayes (he/him) Lighting Designer

Simon Hayes is a Scottish-based lighting designer who has worked with a variety of companies including the National Theatre of Scotland, Royal Lyceum Theatre Edinburgh, Tron Theatre, Citizens Theatre, Beacon Arts, Snap Elastic, Royal Conservatoire of Scotland, Edinburgh International Festival, Dandelion Festival, Jordan and Skinner and Glass Performance. He enjoys collaborating to produce thought-provoking, stimulating and evocative lighting designs (as well as the occasional bit of joy and silliness).

Credits include: *Pride & Prejudice* (sort of)* (Royal Lyceum Theatre); *Yellow Canary* (GLASS Performance); *Moonset* (Citizens Theatre); *The Time Machine* (Jordan & Skinner); *Eat Me* (Snap Elastic); *Shift* (National Theatre of Scotland); *The Motherf***er with the Hat* (Tron Theatre).

Simon Liddell (he/him) Composer and Musician

Simon Liddell is a regular in the Scottish music scene, a multi-instrumentalist, forming and playing in numerous bands (Olympic Swimmers/Owl John) before joining Frightened Rabbit in 2013, touring extensively and releasing via Atlantic Records. He has since performed and recorded with artists including Paws, Gretta Ray, The Vaselines and Poster Paints. 2018 saw his first venture into theatre, collaborating with Gary McNair on *McGonagall's Chronicles*, before scoring *After the Cuts* and *Square Go* (Fringe First winner, and nominated for a Drama Desk Award) at the Edinburgh Fringe. Recent theatre work includes Henry Naylor's *Games* (Arcola Theatre/Adelaide Fringe), *Whatever Happened to the Jaggy Nettles* (Citizens Theatre), "The Domestic" (NTS/Scenes for Survival), and *Strange Rocks?* (Mull Theatre).

Gary McNair (he/him) Writer and Performer

Gary McNair is a writer-performer based in Glasgow.

He aims to make work that will challenge and entertain audiences in equal measure. His work has been translated into several languages and been performed around the world from America to Australia, from Germany to Japan, and from Portugal to Possilpark. He is a mainstay of the Edinburgh Fringe where his last seven shows have sold out and he has won the coveted Scotsman Fringe First Award three times.

He is an Associate Artist at both Traverse Theatre in Edinburgh and Tron Theatre in Glasgow. He loves telling stories and is delighted that people want to hear them.

Recent works include: *Dear Billy* (National Theatre of Scotland); *Nae Expectations* (Tron); *Jekyll and Hyde* (Reading Rep/Lyceum); *Black Diamonds and the Blue Brazil* (Lyceum); *The Alchemist* (Tron); *Square Go* (co-authored by Kieran Hurley) (Francesca Moody Productions/ Paines Plough); *McGonagall's Chronicles* (Òran Mór); *Locker Room Talk/Letters to Morrissey/Donald Robertson Is Not a Standup Comedian* (Traverse); *A Gambler's Guide to Dying* (Show and Tell/ Traverse).

Jill O'Sullivan (she/her) Composer and Musician

Jill O'Sullivan is a Glasgow-based multi-instrumentalist/singer/ songwriter/composer who writes and performs across the worlds of popular music, theatre and dance. Since releasing three critically acclaimed albums with her band Sparrow and the Workshop (formed in 2008), Jill has gone on to collaborate with a multitude of renowned musicians and perform at prestigious music festivals and venues throughout the United Kingdom and Europe. She recently released a full-length album under the name Jill Lorean and will be releasing new music in 2024.

ABOUT NATIONAL THEATRE OF SCOTLAND

National Theatre of Scotland is a Theatre Without Walls.

We don't have our own venue; instead, we're able to bring theatre to you wherever you are. From the biggest stages to the smallest community halls, we showcase Scottish culture at home and around the world. We have performed in airports and tower blocks, submarines and swimming pools, telling stories in ways you have never seen before.

We want to bring the joy of theatre to everyone.

Since we were founded in 2006, we have produced hundreds of shows and toured all over the world.

We strive to amplify the voices that need to be heard, tell the stories that need to be told and take work to wherever audiences are to be found.

For the latest information on all our activities, visit us online at: nationaltheatrescotland.com

Jackie Wylie (she/her) Artistic Director & Chief Executive
Brenna Hobson (she/her) Executive Director
Jane Spiers (she/her) Chair

To find out about the full team at National Theatre of Scotland please visit: nationaltheatrescotland.com/about/who-we-are/our-people

NTS is proud to be an organisation where all are welcome, and we've listed the pronouns of the cast and creative team in this play text as part of our ongoing commitment to use more inclusive language wherever we can as part of our LGBT Charter for Business Award.

The National Theatre of Scotland is core funded by the Scottish Government.

National Theatre of Scotland, a company limited by guarantee and registered in Scotland (SC234270) is a registered Scottish charity (SC033377).

SUPPORT NATIONAL THEATRE OF SCOTLAND

Did you know the National Theatre of Scotland is a registered charity? To do what we do, we need your support!

Our wonderful donors and supporters have helped us nurture and develop the careers of hundreds of actors, playwrights, designers and directors and create extraordinary work like *Dear Billy* to tour across Scotland and beyond.

We aim to break down the walls that prevent people from engaging with our work, whether economic, cultural or physical. Each year we develop projects with young people to build confidence and transform lives.

There are so many ways you can support and be part of our work to create inclusive, vital and dynamic theatre.

To learn more, please visit: nationaltheatrescotland.com/support.

DEAR BILLY – WRITER'S NOTE

It's such a genuine honour and delight to be making this show for you. To say that I am excited about it would be an understatement. That's not to say that the last few years haven't been without the occasional moment of waking up in the night thinking: 'What the hell are we doing? You don't take on the Big Yin, that's sacred stuff!' But yet somehow, here we are.

This show has been a long time in the making. How long? Well, you could say it's been in development a few years. Or when the first of many people said to me, 'You should do a show about Billy Connolly!'

Or back to twenty-five years ago when I was stood in the stairwell at school listening to a tape of the Jobby Weecha for the first time, totally captivated, lost in the moment and pishing myself laughing, completely unaware that the bell had rung long ago.

As I've embarked further into this project I've come to realise that I, and anyone else who is lucky enough to tell stories on stage for a living, owes a huge debt of gratitude to Billy for blazing a trail as wide as the Clyde and leaving plenty of room in his wake for people to find their own voice and use it.

Often when someone makes a show where they are the writer and performer, people can assume that it is a 'solo work' or a 'one-man show'. That's not what this is. Sure I'm up there telling the stories. But there are two other performers with me for a start and then the director of a show like this is much more of a co-pilot than anything else. Music plays such a big part of telling these stories, as does the design, and then there's all the creatives, technicians and producers that have made this show with our National Theatre. And of course there is the incredible team of story gatherers and researchers who spoke to countless people around Scotland. And finally, the people across Scotland themselves. Without their generosity with their time and their stories, this show would not be possible. It has been a joy to work with these stories.

I only wish we could share them all with you.

Gary McNair (Writer/Performer), May 2023

Dear Billy

For Katy, Rosa, Leo

& Billy

The stage is set.

We are somewhere between a pub/club/ephemeral space that captures the spirit of Billy:

Three striking neons, which each represent part of his iconography, adorn the space. The first neon takes the shape of his signature glasses; these hang in the centre of the space in front of an open purple curtain. Stage left there is a neon welly boot which forms a table and on stage right there is a glorious neon banana which forms a chair.

Behind the banana is the band's station.

Uplifting preshow music plays.

The band enter and take their instruments.

They treat us to a beautiful violin and guitar rendition of 'Everybody Knows That' by the Humblebums. As the song is just about to go into the chorus . . .

Gary *enters.*

Gary SHUT IT!

The band stop abruptly; they laugh. **Gary** *turns to the audience with a big smile and his arms open wide. Reciprocating any warmth from the crowd in a way that says clearly, 'Thanks for having us, I can't wait!'.*

Gary Hello, how are you doing?

It's so nice to be here, thanks for having us.

Oh, just a wee bit of house business before we go any further. If anyone is sat there absolutely gutted, devastated beyond belief, the arse is just shat out the back of them with disappointment at the fact that *this* is the face that has just walked out to meet them and not that of Billy Connolly
I'm sorry.
The marketing has failed you
If you don't think you will be able to get over that level of disappointment I will understand if you want to take this opportunity to leave

Please do speak to a member of staff on your way out where a full refund will be . . . politely declined

Looks out to check no one is leaving.

Oh good, we're not going to have another 'Dundee' on our hands.

OK, with that said, let me tell you:

We have been so lucky to have been going around the country
Over the last few years
With our tape recorders.
Talking to people about the Big Yin
Collecting people's Billy Connolly stories
We've been all over,
We've met all sorts.
And I really mean . . . All sorts.

We've met plenty of:
'Oh Ah love him''s

We've had more than a few:
'Ah'm his biggest fan!'

We've met people who owe their sense of humour,
their sense of identity,
their very sense of self to this man

We've met quite a lot of:
'Oh, Ah'd leave ma husband fur him''s.

Here, we've also hud a few:
'Ah'd leave ma wife fur him''s

We have had a few, I've got to be honest, we've had a few:
'I don't really like him''s

Aye.
Honest.
I told you. We met *all* sorts.

We've even met a, and you're no gonna believe this but Ah swear to God we even met a:

'Sorry . . . Billy who? . . . Connolly? Nope, doesn'y ring a bell.'

Yup. We even found *that* guy!

We. Have. Had. It. All.

I'd love it if we could bring you them all.
I'd love to bring all those voices.
All those stories.
They're all rich and beautiful, funny, warm, heartbreaking, tender and complex in all their own wee joyous ways

But if we were to do that, the show would run at about twelve hours and no one would thank us for that.
Least of all the band.

So, instead what we are going to bring you is our best attempt to piece the man together
From those voices
From those stories
Bringing you all the unique ways, the big and the small, that he matters to . . . us.
And maybe learn something about ourselves along the way.

All the words you'll hear tonight are real words from real people.

This is the Big Yin, according to the people of Scotland, in their own words

The show has expanded as we have been on the road, as we've met more beautiful people like yourself and collected more Billy Connolly stories.
And it will continue to evolve as we travel with the show,
Because wherever you go in the world, you'll find people,
And wherever there are people,
There are people who are happy to talk about the Big Yin.

A shift.

Music starts.

Gary *heads to the back of the stage where there is a piece of card on a stool. He turns the card over, and appears to read what's on the other side as if he is checking a set list or running order. He turns the card back over, writing face down, and heads to the front of the stage.*

As he approaches one of the mics, he does so like he doesn't know what it is or is at least hesitant to speak into it.

He is now a member of the public. A member of the public who is surprised and delighted to be asked their opinion of Billy.

Biggest Fan

Here is that no unbelievable! Sorry, do I just talk into your wee tape hingwy?
Right. Sorry, I said is that no unbelievable?
You're out here the day talking tae folk about Billy Connolly.
And here's me, only his biggest fan!
Aye, oh aye. I love him to bits. I love everything he does.
And I tell you what, I actually do quite a good Billy Connolly as well.
Yes, I do!
Aye, I'm no bad.
'Come on,' yer sayin, 'just bloody do it.'
OK, OK, OK, but I'm nervous, you know, cause
Ah've aw talked masel up.
But even my ma family aw say I'm good and they're usually first tae tell me Ah'm shite at something so . . .
Oh, awright, 'Enough, enough, just get on we it.' Right, ah

(*Clears throat, composes themself, makes a beginnings of a sound.*)

Ah but you're looking right at me noo, and that's makin' me awfy nervous,
you've got to . . . here, close your eyes would you, eh?
Cause . . . aye cause then you can picture him in yer heed and no ma weird wee puss.

Right, have you got your eyes closed?
You'll pure tell me it's pish but Ah'm just gonna dae it anyway. Right. Here goes.
'Ohh hellooooo, its meeeee, Billyyyyyyy, Billy Con'llyyyy.'
Was that no alright?

Gary *moves to another mic where he will become someone else. This will continue now for the rest of the show. For every new speaker, a new mic. Each character is given a name, e.g. 'Too Much' – these are for reference and not to be read out.*

Montage One

1 *Too Much*

So you're telling me the things Ah say to you about Billy Connolly
Into this wee tape hingwy
Could be said
On a stage
By an actor
Aw that's . . . that's . . .
Aw that's too much pressure, man!

2 *I Wish*

Billy Connolly?
Oh I am too young for him . . . I wish!

3 *Friends wi Royalty*

Aye and he's friends wi royalty as well, ain't he?
Aye.
But we'll no hold that against him

4 *Best Man on Two Feet*

He's the best man on two feet.
He is a man. He is a big man.
Aye, Ah think there should be a wee sta'ue eh him round here.

Or up the town.
Him and Andy Murray.
Aye the two eh them together, aye.
Aw but listen, he is a man. He is a big man

5 *Fifty Pence*

Fufty Pence Ah paid to go and see him.
He was garbage
We got up and walked out
Ach he was just startin' out
We were just there to support
But was that no a load eh money back then, 50 pence?
Would Ah pay 50 pence to see him now?
Naw.
Naw, naw, listen, I'd pay a lot more than that, aye.

6 *Chips*

Ah threw chips at him.
Ah said, 'Ah threw chips at him.'
Had on, fuck, is this thing recordin'?!

7 *Ah'll Chat about Him!*

Here listen, mate
I'm no wantin' tae talk tae anyone about anyhin'
Sling yer fuckin' (hook)
Oh, Billy Connolly?
Oh aye, Ah'll chat about him!
Aye, nae worries at all
Sit doon, aye, what d'ye want to ask?

8 *Back End eh Beyond*

That man could rock up in the farthest-flung regions
eh the Baltics
or the Bahamas,
or Botswana,
or the . . . fuckin' back end eh beyond,

and folk'd be lit
'Fuck me. Is that the Big Yin?!'

9 *Pishing in the Sink*

Aw ma da's records were aw the same:
This wan in a jumper
This wan in a cardigan
An' then BAM!
Along comes this wan
And he's got the dark beard
The big hair
The skinny jeans
Banana boots
Smokin' a fag and pishin' into the sink
And Ah'm thinkin'
'Oh aaaaye. Ah want tae know more about this guy!'

10 *Judi Dench*

Oh aye, he was good in that wan wi eh . . .
Wi . . . that. Judi Dench
Aye that eh . . .
Mrs Brown's Boys

11 *Did He Play for Rangers?*

You want me to tell you about Billy Connolly?
Nah sorry, man, I've got nothing on him
Did he . . . Did he used tae play for rangers, did he?

Ach Ah'm pullin' yer pisser.
Of course Ah know who the Big Yin is!
D'ye hink Ah'm fae the moooon or su'hin.

12 *Funniest Man in the World, Man*

Aw, man.
That man is the funniest man
In the world, man!

Apart fae meeeee!

13 *Wan eh Us*

Billy Connolly?
Aw, he's a man eh the people . . .
even though he's got the mansions,
and the castle, fuck me,
But he is, he's just lit an honest tae goodness normal guy.
Well, no normal, lit, abnormal but like in the nicest possible way.
He's just absolutely wan eh us

The montage music comes to a big finish.

Gary *heads back up to the stool and checks in once again with the writing on the back of the card before carrying on with the show, continuing to go from mic to mic as he becomes each new person.*

Wee. Poor. Glasgow.

Wee.
Poor.
Glasgow.

Right, that about covers it. You can get away up the the road.

Nah there's more than that.
Ah mean we were aw getting bashed about and battered
That wis normal
But Ah think he had it a bit worse than the rest of us.
Mum left. Auntie was a monster. Dad was a monster. It was TERRIBLE.
Ah mean he didny complain like, but like, who was he gonnae complain too?

Teachers?! Fuck me, THEY WERE WORSE!

You'd be lit that:

'Excuse me, miss, I just wanted to make you aware of the violence at home.'

They'd be lit that:

'You what? Get out ma sight, ya waste of skin.' WALLOP!

'Actually, come back here.' WALLOP! WALLOP!

Ye'd be lit that:

'Ah. What was that one for?'

'Being glaiket. Now, get oot!'

How It Was

Ah know you're standin' there, big fella, thinkin', 'How? A life of depravity, abandonment and beatings, *how* could that feel normal?' But then you never grew up in Glasgow in the 1950s, did ye?

Similar Upbringing

I had, eh, I had quite a similar upbringing to him and I didn't like that people made me feel like I couldn't complain. Ye know, they'd all say things like, 'Well, at least you had a home', to try and shut me up, ye know? And, well, he got that as well, didn't he, when they said all that about his book, how they were saying, 'You cannae say that about your auntie, at least she took you in.' And then he said something. And it really got me. It really got me.
He said: 'I hate it, I *hate* it, when people are generous in the moment and they make you pay for it the rest of your life'. That really stuck wi me.

You Cannae Treat a Child Like That

Oh no no no
You, you, you canna treat a child like that.
No.
Never.
It's a child, by Christ.

A child needs to be . . . nurtured . . . supported . . . encouraged . . . loved . . . Even the glaikit ones.

Helped Make Him

Now for some folk that violence would breed violence. Right, like, ma da was a prick, right. And he blamed that on the fact that *his* da was a prick.
So by that logic, the Big Yin had every right to swan about like a prick and blame his upbringing. But he didny do that. It's almost as if he wouldn't ever want to make anyone feel the way he had been made to feel.

Now, I'm no saying that makes it worthwhile. That all that suffering was the price to pay to become who he was, ye know.

Naw, fuck that, man, that's deal wi the devil stuff that. If a happy child makes a boring adult, well, then gie me a world full eh borin' adults, any day of the week – absolutely. But, as a says, seein' as he did suffer as a waen and that he did go on to bring so much joy to the world. Well, does that no make him . . . pretty special?

Connections

Naw naw naw, as Ah said, Ah don't remember him

Naw

I know he grew up round here somewhere, like, ye know. But I dinnae remember him personally fae back then.

Loads ah boys ah cut about wi say they do, lit, remember him, like, like fae back then.

But, honestly, Ah, Ah . . . I think they're talkin' pish.

Aye, naw, honestly. I do.

Cause ye get a lot eh folk aw goin'

'Aw here, ma sister' or 'Ma brother was in his year at school'.

And sure, right, maybe some eh them were.

Cause obviously he must eh had *some* folk in his actual class.
But . . . ye meet an away lot eh them, don't ye?

Wi some of them it's like:
'Oh, aye, eh . . . ma wee brother was in his class.'

Even though you know fine well, just by lookin' at this guy,
that he's clearly a good ten year younger than the Big Yin.
And so his wee brother must eh been even younger than that.
Cause that's . . . how it works. Ye know.

But folk like tae make a wee connection don't they?
Like, they want to feel . . . connected to things.

It's like how when folk pass on a story,
ye know,
and they're no sure if its true or no but they want it to be true,
now, the Big Yin, he would just be lit that:
'Ah hope tae God this is true'
and then he'd tell ye and you'd make up your own mind.
But people dinnae dae that, they tend tae add . . . a wee claim tae it,
they try and make it, lit, more authentic,
so they'll, ye know, they'll tell you it happened tae someone they know. Ye know, they tend tae go:
'Oh it happened tae ma . . . neighbour' right? Or 'ma sister' or 'ma cousin' kinda hing.
Oh never themselves, no. Naw, cause then you could ask follow-up questions

'WHIT?! A dug was drivin' a Ford Fiesta was it? My God. What colour was it?'

'Eh . . . purple.'

'Funny colour for a dug.'

So it's always, 'Ma brother . . . my brother's wife . . . ma brother's wife's auntie's budgie was there. Ah swear!'

But I didn't know him. Not knowingly. I didn't knowingly know him. Not that I know of. You know?

Kids Ran Wild

But look, anyway, in the hoose would have been shite for him. But, oot and aboot? They had the run of the place.
Him and his half a million wee classmates
Whoever they all were.

But it was great runnin' about Glasgow back then.
Cause you really could dae whit ye wanted.
Cause ye see,
The men were aw in the pubs drunk.

And the women were aw at home . . . drunk!

So the streets belonged to the weans. The streets . . . of Partick!

No Govan. Partick

Now listen here. Look, ah see your face and you're thinking 'fuck ye talkin' about? He's no fae Partick, he's fae Govan!'
He's no fae fuckin' Govan.
A lot of people think he's fae Govan, but he's NO fae Govan.
He's frae Partick!
Over . . . There!
He's . . . you know . . . wan ay *them*.

To be fae Govan, tae be a *real* Govanite, you need to have been born under the cran and dragged through the Elder pond. Right? Well, was he? Was he? Was he fuck.

Nah, he was only in Govan two minutes.
He's no fae Govan.
Partick. He's. Fae. Partick.

What Is Partick?

Now 'What is Partick?' I hear you cry. 'What splendorous wonderland is that?'

Ok . . . How to describe Partick?

Right. Picture a quaint wee village on the outskirts of Glasgow, carved out from hill and glen. A serene wee getaway that's a haven from the hustle and bustle of the industrial grind of the city itself.

Actually, quaint doesn't quite cover it.

Serene? Absolutely

Tranquil? A hundred per cent

Idyllic.

Right, hawd that image there. Picture it in your mind. Now, I want you to replace that image with a shithole at the back of the town.

Now, I must stress, I'm no saying that it's any more of a shithole that the rest of the town. I actually happen to quite like Partick. But it's just tenements and hills. Fuckin' HILLS everywhere.
It's kinda like those streets in San Francisco in all the movies but . . . shite.

Naw listen. I like Partick. I do.
Partick is like . . . a cheese piece, ye know?
Like it's no fancy.
It's just lit, ye know what ah mean.
Like if someb'dy gave ye a cheese piece fur yer dinner ye'd be lit,
'Fuck sake, that's a shite dinner.' But then actually, ye know, you'd tuck in and be lit, 'Here, actually, that was fuckin' magic, ye know, just what ah needed!'

NO it was FINE. Loads of fun! Just shite fun you had to invent yourself. Like chasing folk. Or getting a chase off someone. Or watching a chase.

Aw naw listen. Good people. Good neighbours. The lot. It would have done him well to grow up in a place like Partick.

Right on the Clyde

It's right on the Clyde. And its main trades are fish and hunting. By which I mean there's about a hundred chippies and you should watch out for people wi knives.

God you wouldny eat a fish out the Clyde. Christ! You see them though, those guys, don't you? Stood at the edge of the Clyde with the fishing rod, between two tug boats and oil spill and I said, 'What kind eh a fish you think you're gonna catch here?'

And he looks up and says:

'You can judge all you want but I'll be the one who'll be able to survive the apocalypse.'

'Apocalypse?! Keep eatin' that and you'll be lucky to survive the summer!'

Never Forgot

He never forgot where he came fae . . . Anderston.

The tone shifts here – we return to the lighting state and delivery mode from the prologue. This should help make it clear that this story is not from a member of the public like the others so far, but is in fact **Gary** *the performer's personal story. Like, the prologue, it is not delivered into a mic.*

Gary One

Now, you might be sitting there wondering
'Gary, Gary, have you ever met him?'
Well, let me tell you a story, right.
I was sitting in a wee Glasgow cafe, having a wee bit of lunchity crunch, a wee soupçon, a wee . . . well, probably a roll and sausage.
Point is, ma phone goes, right
And it's ma mate, Ah've no heard from him in ages, Ah'm like:
'Oh hi, how you doing?'
And he's like:
'Guess who's here?'
And I'm like:
'I don't know where you are, start wi that'
So he tells me and I still don't know so I say:
'Just tell me.'
And he says:
'He is walking amongst us, bold as brass, gallus as ye like, acting like he is *not* the Big Yin.'
And I'm like:
'The Big Yin? Fuckin' lead with that! Right, keep him there!'
And he's like:
'Who the fuck do you think I am?! You get here as soon as you can.'
And I was lit that, right, fuck, right eh, fuck it
And grabbed my things and Ah darted for the door of the cafe
But then I was like, 'Shit, Ah've no paid!'
So I was just lit:
'Here, mate, I'm sorry, I'm no running away without paying, I need to go right now, but I swear I'll come back and pay later, right, I swear. Look at ma face. Look at my face. I'll be back and pay but I need to go.'
Probably thought I'd shat myself or someone had died or something.
But either way I am off.

Bursting a lung on my bike, hoofin' it across town.
I get there, dart inside and see ma pal
'Is he still here? Is he still here?!'
But before he can even answer, I already know. Cause I can tell.
I can feel him
I'm no kiddin'
There is a presence
And there he is sat there in some kind eh glow
Ye know?
With the aura
Aw roon'

There is a shift in tone. We are once back to hearing from members of the public.

Never Forgets

Ay naw but look, wherever he is fae, lit inside eh Glasgow, he is he *from* Glasgow
bor . . . bur . . . bre . . . born and raised in Glasgow . . .
Never forgets who he is.
Never lost his accent
Even although he's livin' in America noo, I think it's . . . eh, Monte Carlo?
Ach, Somewhere in America anyway
But
He's *still* got his Scottish accent
Never forgets where he is
You know?
Where he's from.
In there. (*Points to heart.*)

Gary *slowly makes his way off the stage through the upstage curtains as the band plays a lovely rendition of 'Ramblin' Boy' by Tom Paxton.*

Gary *re-enters in outlandish bright clothes adorned with bananas and drawings of the Big Yin.*

He joins the last chorus of 'Ramblin' Boy' on the kazoo with the objective to play it so brashly that the song falls apart, either by stealing the show or, preferably, by making Jill laugh when she's trying to sing.

Gary *returns to the mics to be more members of the public.*

AH Cleaned His Bothy

'Oh I knew him'
'Ah stayed in the same building as him'
'Ah solt him his first fiddle'
'Ah battered him'
'Ah made him laugh'
'Ah get off wi him'
'He gee'd ma sister impetigo!'
Ye know, kind eh hing?

But Ah did. Ah actually did.
Ah worked in the yards wi him.

But Ah swear down, my hand to God, Ah worked wi him. Ah cleaned his bothy!

Aye, twenty-one year Ah were in the British shipbuilders.
Yeah I cleaned aw eh their owffices.
Fae the high up tae the low doon.
And then I hud to go aw the way down to the end eh that road and clean aw they mingin', manky, mockit bothies
Ah hud tae clean his boggy bottin' bu . . . bu . . . place.
Rotten!
So it wis.
Absolutely rotten.
You ask him, see if he denies it
He willnae.
Cause he couldn'y.
Cause it was.

Saw Him Coming but He Got Gallus

Oh we saw him coming in there though.
Aw peely Wally wi the big hair and the wee pubes on his chin and we've thought
'Right, we're geein' this wan the runaroond'

Of course, those were the days when they'd send you straight from the schoolyard to the dockyard. Wipe your arse and stick you in a pair of overalls.

And he's that delighted to be there he's running about trying get them aw the things they've asked fur; a long stand, tartan paint and aw that.
Pure gullible. But he found his own way through it. Got pure gallus.
Wis never gonna batter any of them for what they got up tae.
Naw he was fuckin' tiny. So he went on the wind-up.
He just becomes the funniest fucker in the place.
Come tea break instead eh us aw rippin' the pish oot eh him, he's goat us aw gathered roon pishin oorsells at aw his routines and the pure gallus singin and aw that.
Aw 'Heedy Haw Aaaww Heedy Haaaw'.
Aw he was the best. Didn'y act it though. Didn'y act aw the big fella, or the smart arse or anythin', he was funny as fuck and he knew it, but he was just wan eh us, ye know? You'll see him, there's pictures eh him, right in amongst us, big Jimmy Reid's talkin' tae us, must eh been the work-in or something like that, and there he is, BANG, Ah'm about three behind him, look it up, you'll see it.
I tell you what though, there was a lot of guys wasted in that place, I don't mean on the (*mimes drinking a bottle*) mind you there was a lot eh us needed a swift one or four before we got up some eh they heights wi out any eh yer modern safety apparatus, ye know?
But Ah mean a lot eh them should eh been poets, writers, thinkers, artists ye know?
If you want to see an artefact lost to the annals of history, you want to have seen the toilet doors in that place. See if you

made that toilet door, my friend you had made it. And I think he made it a wee bit beyond the toilet door, aye. Aye he was the best, man.

Shite at Weldin'

It's a good thing he could get a laugh out ah folk
Ye know, because Ah tell you what,
if he wis as good at comedy as he wis at weldin'
then he'd eh been shite at comedy.
Coz he wis . . . he wis shite at weldin'.

Wan eh 'Them'

Oh I think he got a wee bit eh a hard time off some eh the guys down the shipyards. Cause he wis, well . . . I think it wis . . . well because he wis, ye know, a wee bit, ye know . . . *wan ae 'them'* . . . aye . . . you know . . . well, he wis a . . .
a . . . a . . .
Well, he wis . . . aye . . . a, well, aye, you know . . . a . . .
ca. tho. lic.
Aye. Aye, he might still be. Aye.
But ye know, he won them over, I hink. Most eh them.

Aye, well, he was a very funny ca . . . ca . . . character so he wis. Aye.
Naw, naw I'd, I'd no hold that against him, naw.
Others wid, mind you, and ah think that's a shame.
Cause he's . . . he's no like the rest eh them.
Naw, very funny. Aw aye, awfy funny. Aye.

Song – 'Fuck Him':

Down in a Partick boozer
On a Tuesday afternoon
Theres a group eh four
Bitter bald wee men
Just drinkin', sitting aroon

They've talked about how Catholics
Should not be in their work
Now someone's mentioned Connolly
And there's a big chorus eh fuckin'
fuck him
Aye fuck him

Ach he's awrite
His patter's shite

He's a wee bit eh hem
He's wan eh them

SO fuck him
Ayeeee fuck him

He used to be funny now he just jumps about the scuzz
He's no writ a word, he nicked aw his patter fae us

Any Wan eh Us Could eh Done That

Ach any wan eh us could eh done what he did!
There was loads ah funny guys down there.
Really funny.
He wasny actually that funny
No really.
Naw he didny like, come up wi it, ye know.
He just kind ah . . . pit it all thigither.
Aye, there was loads eh folk were as funny as that
He just nicked it aw fae them.

Aye, you mark ma words, we were aw funny.
Aye, maself included!
Aye,
Aye, absolutely!
Alright then, here's one . . . what do ye . . . naw, ah mean . . . eh . . . how many . . . eh naw, em . . . there's a guy and he's got . . . eh, whit's he . . . naw, here whit was that one wi the . . .?

Well, look, naw ah cannae . . . mind, but . . . aye, any wan eh us could eh done what he done!

Ma Brother

You meet them, though, don't you? People that don't like Connolly.
I am afraid to say my ayn brother is wan eh they people.
Can ye imagine?
He says it's 'rude'.
Ah don't know. Ma ayn brother?!
My ayn flesh and blood.
Ah'm startin' tae think there was maybe foul play,
Ye know, maybe when ma da was away wi the army
Do you know what ah mean?
Cause otherwise, how could Ah be brothers wi that?
Anyway, as Ah say, it takes all sorts don't it . . . tae . . .
And he is . . .
Right, see . . . ye ever seen, you'd eh seen this before, right,
At some point in yer life,
These guys that,
When they go to bogs,
The urinals, right
And . . . when they, no that yer watching,
But ye cannae but help no see, ye know, when they're pishin' at the urinal,
Right, some folk,
instead eh just whippin' the old pipe out,
they actually fuckin' pull their trousers down,
lit awe the way doon,
Like tae their ankles!
It's rare but you'll eh seen them out in the wild, aye?
Maybe once or twice, Aye?
Aye. Aye, well, *that's* ma brother.
That's who doesn't like Connolly.

Folk Tradition

Aw listen ye meet some guys that'll say, 'Aw, he just nicked aw his jokes fae the yards'
But, I'm no having that. Ah'm no havin' that at aw.
That was the tradition, ye know, the folk tradition
Fuckin' . . . folk weren'y headin' up the road after the whistle went so they could sit up awe night at their desks wi a fuckin' . . . pen and paper
Or a, a fuckin' . . . typewriter
Trying to craft the perfect joke.
Naw! They heard aw fae other folk, in the pub or whatever and then they told their pals and hoped they hadny heard it before. That's why they say, 'Did you hear the one about . . .'
D'ye know what Ah mean?
He took aw that . . . aw they wee bits 'n' bobs and jokes and stories and that and carried the culture on to the next town. Like the bards of old ye know. But like instead eh just telling them to the other folk at work, he told people on a stage or up on telly or whatever. Just so happened he became huge. Cause, ye know, he took that . . . made it something that no one else could eh.
It still felt like you were gettin' told it down the pub, just better than anyone down the pub could ever tell it. Ye know?
Ach ye get some bitter old clowns that are annoyed wi that.
But whit ye gonna do?

Miserable

Oh but listen, he was funny. And Ah mean . . . funny.
But that's good though, ain't it?
It's good tae laugh.

Aye ye need a laugh sometimes don't ye? You do.
Aye cause otherwise you could end up . . . miserable.

Can Ah Say Cunt?

But look, there were a lot eh good folk in there
I mean some eh them were mad as fuck, but ye know
And some real funny cunts. Aw fuck can ah say cunt?
Ach, well, aye, you know what I'm saying. Lit that they were good cunts. No lit . . . *cunts*. You know?

But listen, naw, like he would say that as well, though, wouldn't he? That you're no calling some cunt a cunt just cause you're calling them a cunt. Every cunt knows that, right?

Gary *sits down on the banana chair and speaks to the band in the character from this scene.*

One Night in Paisley

Let's have a wee change of tempo, would it be possible to play something with a bit more of a bop to it?

The band do this.

Aw thanks. That's marvellous. Oh that fair takes me back.

He addresses the audience again.

Right. Well, apparently it started one night in Paisley. He was doin' some songs and, ye know people often overlook that, ye know his song singing part of who he was, ye know the contribution he made to the folk culture. See if he got struck by a bus in 1971 I think we'd still be talking about the contribution he made to the folk culture. Of course everybody remembers 'The Welly Boot Song' that he made famous of course, aye, everybody knows that, absolutely, everybody knows that. But what about his other songs like erm . . . well, like erm . . . like 'Everybody Knows That', which ironically not so many people do. And that one about the donkey. I love it! And a bang up-to-date political alaga . . . alga . . . algara . . . alagum, eh . . . alalgoryth . . . algahingy, for the times we are in. Ye know?

Anyway, he was in Paisley. And he was doing a folk song, big long thing about a boat or a whale or a whale on a boat. Or something. Anyway, he forgets the words. Aye, he forgets the words! And rather than let it bother him or it making him panic or get him vexed or stressed, he decides to just go wi the flow. He's pure gallus so he is so he just goes 'I've forgotten the words but here's what the song's about' and the audience are aw pissin' theirsells.

But is that no just pure Glasgow eh? They're like that down there, aren't they? 'I don't know the words but, fuck it, I'll gee you an even better time just coming up wi ma own wee mad version eh the thing.' Fuckin' brilliant. That is pure Glasgow, is it no? It's like those guys that took old things and made them better, you know . . . what's their name? . . . Wombles! That's it. But better than than them. And they weren'y fae Glasgow. But you know what I mean. Like a big Glasgow, comedy Womble. But like . . . better.

He was just, you know, he arrived on the scene like nothin' else. He just did his own thing, irrespective of what other people were doing. A free spirit. Like . . . well, like a Womble!
But you know, no that.

But anyway. That night in Paisley. Something happened. And there was no turnin' back.

Some Baws

Imagine leavin' the shipyards to go sing songs. That takes some baws. Din't it?
That's what it took tae day that. A big heavy pair of hairies.

Chip Pan

I'll never forget him on Parky. You know, the Parkinson show. Whatever they called it. And he told that joke. Fuckin' hell man. Here's this guy, nobody's ever heard eh him. He doesn't look like embody else on the telly, he doesn't *sound* like anybody else on the telly, the only way you were getting on the telly when you sound like him is if you were . . . wearing a See-You-Jimmy hat or if you were good at football or darts or if you were leading a miners' strike or your family had died in a chip-pan fire, you know? And yet here he is: 'Haw, you, aye, you at home. Sit up and listen!' And he tells that joke about the dead wife and the bike and his manager's like that 'Don't you tell that joke' and he was like 'Aw I quite want tae tell that joke' and he was like 'Don't you tell that fuckin' joke!' And he was like 'Oh ok ok, I'll no tell the joke'. Man, he was always going to tell that joke!

He saw his opportunity, he grabbed it with both hands and he set the world on fire. Nothing was ever the same again. For him. Or the rest ay us.

This Place Can Crush Ye

Aw but listen, if I'd ah heard he was leaving to do it full time I'd Ah had a quiet word in his ear, bless him. There were better singers about the yards. Well, there were better singers in the mortuary, by Christ. But I guess he must eh just had that thing in him and that made him think, 'You know what? Ah'm gonna have to fuckin' . . . do this.'
And that's no easy.
No round here, you know.
This place can . . . it can . . . ye know . . . take your positivity and crush it.

Oh don't get me wrong it's a beautiful place and the people are marvellous. But folk roon here can be quick to shut you the fuck up if you try and be a bit different.
Ma cousin grew a beard about 1973. Right? And he got such a fuckin' hard time that he shaved it off a week later and people, to this day, still call him Mr Big Shot. Just to keep him down. You know? Just tae say, 'Don't even bother, mate.'

'Just you get back in line.'
A fuckin' beard, by Christ!
You know? What would we have been robbed of if the bastards had dragged *him* doon enough to stop him fae being who he was, tae keep him at the grind. Who knows who else this city's crushed, people who didny have whatever he had that made him go, 'Fuck it, I'm gonna do this, I'm gonna gee it a go.'
At least we got him.

Gary *checks in with the piece of card on the stool once again.*

It is clear that we have again returned to **Gary***'s personal story and he is picking from where we left off in* **Gary One**.

Gary Two

Of course, you'll remember, he is sitting with the aura aw aroon'.
Now, to be fair, he was being interviewed for the telly so there was a lot of big bright lights on him. But I swear he still shone out from the middle eh it.
And I'm thinking, 'Oh my God there he is. There he is and I'm here.'
And I'm nervous
I want a triple gin but I realise that would be a very bad idea
But I need something
My mouth's aw dry
I have a big glass eh water but it's got a lot of ice in it and between the ice and the nerves I'm worried I'll sound aw squeaky, ye know?
And so I need something hot, something that'll warm the throat, open the voice, something that's going to open the uvular folds, I know these things cause I'm trained you see.
So Ah have a coffee. And that's great for the cold throat
But it's a fuckin' nightmare for the nerves,
I go absolutely scatty bananas aff ma nut
Pure shakin' and buzzin' away lit fuckin'

Whoooaa
So now I'm like
'What the fuck am I doing?'
What the fuck am I gonna talk about wi him?'
But also getting distracted by like a shiny fork
So I'm like,
'Right, head in the game'
But I'm also like
'I wonder how long it would take to eat a swan?'
So my heed's gone
Brain has absolutely just fuckin' jumped out the window
And I see that the interview is over
And I've got to jump in
But I've got to go about it respectfully ye know
Don't want him to feel like I'm bombarding him
So I gather myself and think about what I'm gonna say
Fuck am I gonna say?
'Here, you ever notice how magnets are mental?'
It's ok, you've got this, just don't be beige, that's what he'd say, just don't be beige, don't be beige, don't be beige.
What the fuck am I gonna say to him?!

Montage Two

1 *What He Wanted When He Wanted*

And Ah tell ye whit, he said what he wanted, when he wanted to whoever the fuck he wanted. The Big Yin wasnae scared eh anyone!

2 *Rock Star*

Aw he was much more eh a . . . rock star, ye know?
He would just boot his way on tae stages and say
'Here I am, you will listen. And you will enjoy!'

3 *Hecklin' His Own Audience*

First time I saw him he was hecklin' his own audience
Ha ha ha

He was fuckin' terrifying, man.
And this poor wee guy in about fourth or fifth row got up to go to the toilet and he was like . . .
'YOU!'
And the whole place came to a standstill
And he went
'HOW DARE YOU GO FOR A PISS WHILE I'M PERFORMIN'!'
Of course now all the attention's focused on the boy like WHAT?
And he's absolutely shitting himself, man, it was amazing.
Ha ha ha
Ah was just there cause Ah was in the air force
Stationed just up the road
And we'd aw heard the crucifixion
but now, we were going to get to hear it live

Angelic music, a big build in anticipation . . .

Greggs Crucifixion

Ah know every word. Every word of the crucifixion. Every single word. 'So there was a misprint in the Bible . . .' Do you want me to go on? Cause I know it all! I do. I can do it just lit him. Well, no just lit him cause, well, there's him away up there and here's me doon here, and if ah could do it just lit him then maybe Ah'd be the wan wi the castle and the big car an aw that, pure jet skiing and dining out wi movie stars. Ah hid a Greggs for ma dinner. So what does that tell ye? Tells ye I'm no as good as him. But I'll gee it a go. Good enough for you here anyway. Here we are then, the Greggs version of the crucifixion.
There wis a misprint, in the Bible. No a lot oh people know that. But actually it aw happened roon there at the Barrowlands instead eh Bethlehem. Aw naw here it was The Gallowgate sure it wis instead eh Bethlehem. Naw . . . Galilee. There's me dain ma own misprints. It's crackin' either way. So they're aw in the pub. The apostles. Ah mean,

can ye imagine? You wouldny get a way wi that noo. The apostles and the disciples aw sat room the pub, ye know. He could just get away wi it cause he was, ye know . . . the Big Yin. He could get away wi anything. But you wouldny get away wi that now, naw. Mind you, a lot ae the stuff goin on noo's too much, would pickle your mind just thinking about some of the stuff ye see noo, they're aw at the shaggin' and calling each other all sorts so they are. Aye we've lost our way a wee bit. But anyway . . . Here they are, the apostles aw sat around the pub and they're aw sat around talking about that they've spelled the place wrong in the Bible but then the Big Yin comes in and I think he's meant ti be Jesus. You know . . . Christ, that is. And he's geein' it aw: 'You've nae idea the day ah've hud. Pure got crucified,' he says, 'Pure had tae carry a big dod-a-wid up a hill' and they went, 'Here you, jaggy bunnet!' That's the best bit. And a canna mind the rest but it's brilliant.

There you go. I bet you didn't think you were gonna get your very own version oh the crucifixion the day, eh?

Maybe they'll put me on Parky next. If he's still, he's no . . . deed, is he?
Aw brilliant. Get me booked in. Maybe do it quick though eh, you know?

Church music plays.

The Church Hated Him but Led Me to Him

'Do not listen to this blasphemer! Do not listen to this evil man. He is headed to the fiery hole below and anyone who listens will be dragged down with him!'

I'm at Sunday school listening to this horrible, miserable, creepy bastard telling us not to listen to this Connolly guy and I'm thinking, 'If he's the opposite of this guy, he might just be my saviour.'
So that was me, up late, Saturday night, Maw and Da passed

out and me, ear against the speaker, pishing myself at this 'evil guy'.

What an advert they were for him. Pure drove me and aw my mates right to him.
But that's the thing wi God though, eh, he moves in mysterious ways, dun't he? Ye know? He's got a plan and he's got a way of helpin' you to see the bigger picture. What really matters, ye know.

He Wis Like Christ

Nah he was more like Christ. Ye know. He wis. He wis like Jesus!
Spittin' verses and and *we* were aw his disciples.
Man. The Big Yin.
Here's him. No hate in him. A dirty mouth. Funny as fuck.
I'm gonna say it – better than Christ. Aye, there you go.
No. Ah'll no take it back!
Look, if we're aw God's children,
which I believe we are,
then Ah hink he did a better job wi the Big Yin than he did wi Christ. Or me! Or any eh the rest eh us. There, Ah've said it. No Ah'll no take it back! So strike me down. Aye.

Correct

I was in a petrol station in Aberdeen one time and I see this big fancy motor out on the forecourt and I'm thinking, 'Who has a motor like that? That's absolutely gorgeous.'
Then I get inside the shop and I hear the cashier's pishin' herself, laughing away and then I realise she's talkin' tae fuckin' Billy Connolly!
And I'm like that 'Shit, fuck' ye don't think these things are gonna happen, ye know, I'm like, 'Fuckin' hell, what am Ah gonna say tae him?' And then it dawns on me that he's gonna finish payin' and then he's gonna have to turn round

and his only way out eh this place to come past me and I'm gonna have tae speak tae him! And I'm thinking 'Oh God' and then I hear her say cheerio and then he says cheerio and he turns round and he walks right toward me and he's looking at me and I just go, 'Aw . . . Jesus Christ!'
And he goes . . .
'Correct!'

Billy Got Me Off the Drink

I'll tell you what Billy did for me.
He got me off the drink.
No personally.
No. He didnae come round the house, boot the door down
And pour a bottle eh Glennmorangie down the sink
Nah.
Like, like, Ah'd wanted tae get aff the drink for years

And Ah'd tried this
And Ah'd tried that
Tried excuses
'Oh am up early, I'm no wantin' to wake up wi the sore head'
'Oh Ah've tae drive early'
'Oh Ah've got diarrhoea'
'It's ma gran's funeral'
Tried them all
Part fae the truth which was that drink
killed me da
Ruined my maw
And Ah was sure Ah wis next
But the more ye excused yersell
The more people roon here
Say tae ye

'Ach whit's wrang, take a drink, go oan'
And Ah'd no have the strength and eventually the pressure'd get tae me

And then Billy.
Billy came along
And said, 'Ye know whit? I am the Big Yin! An' Ah'm no drinkin'!'
'Ah'm just no dain it!'
D'you know what that did fur me?
Gave me a role model

So from then on Ah'd just say 'Ah'm no drinkin''
And if folk would go 'How no?' Or 'Fucksake' or 'You're a wimp' or whatever
I'd go, 'Is the Big Yin a wimp?'
Don't think so!

See I'm a friend of William's right . . . I'm in the programme
And that helps me too
We take it day at a time
And we've to put our faith in God
But they say, 'Don't worry, God doesn'y need tae mean "God", it's just whatever higher power you believe in'
And we'll, that's Connolly for me.
He's ma higher power.
Want te see ma tattoo?
Is it Jesus? Is it Connolly?
You tell me . . .
It's Connolly.

I Have a Wonderful Life

It's not a funny story, it's . . . just erm . . .
About eight years ago when Billy was on his last tour
And he was touring to Edinburgh to the Usher Hall
Erm my husband and I went with other friends to see him
Erm and it was his Parkinson's tour
Because by that time he'd said he had Parkinson's, etc.
And my husband who . . . died about six weeks ago
Had had Parkinson's
For twenty-two years

Erm . . . and erm
So . . . but he was erm determined that he was going to talk to Billy
I guess because of that thing they were saying
That we all feel like we know him
And we all feel like we want to be somebody that is there to support him
You know
He's just got that thing
And so we waited around outside
And right enough
My husband went up to him and he took his hand
And he put his arm around him and he said:
'Don't worry, Billy, Ah've had Parkinson's for fourteen years'
He said
'And I have a wonderful life
And you will too'

And that's my wee story
It was just it was just
And my husband, at his funeral,
At the service, at the back there's a photograph of him and Billy talking
As I said, it's not a funny story but I just wanted to tell you, so there you are.

Well, I Did Alright

My story wi Billy starts thirty years ago erm. Ah was twenty-three, Ah wis a young nun
In the borders

And one day Billy turned up.
He wanted to learn how to meditate
I think he was getting quite stressed out
With his TV life
And his wife Pamela said, 'Get the fuck tae Samee Ling

And learn how to relax.'
So he did.

And we kind of hit it off.
I told him he wasn't funny
Cause I had a bald head and he called me curly. So . . . come on, he deserved it

I bumped into him again at an event in Glasgow
And he sort of came through the crowd
Came up and gave me a hug and went
'Ah knew you'd be here'
And I'm like '. . . awright'
Now at the time I was living in a monastery
And we were talking about karma and compassion.
And I didn't want to sit and talk about it
I wanted to go and do something
So I asked him to sponsor me
And give me money
Ah said, 'Its nothing to you but I want to go on this adventure and do this work in Kathmandu in Nepal'
He wrote me a cheque
And I bought a one-way ticket
And I didn't come back for nine years
Honestly

And what I did with that money and what I got from that
Will last me for the rest of my life
He really really enabled me to go on this amazing adventure
I ran a children's home
I was feeding people
Learned to cook,
the daal that you ate tonight is a direct consequence of me going to Nepal
And eh, working for charity
Paid for people surgeries
And eh . . . it's all down to him

Well, jump to four years ago and I see him on telly
And he's looking quite frail

And I get quite upset
And I think
I have to let him know, I have to let him know what a life-changing experience this was. Not just for me but for all the people I was able to help.

I wanted to thank him and I didn't think he'd remember
He'll get so many people asking for stuff

Anyway it's quite hard to get a hold of people like Billy
but . . . I was working for a kilt makers in Edinburgh
And I found out that the owner's son was going over to America to dress Billy for New York Tartan Week
So I got on a bus
Went right down to his son's shop and I said
'You've got to put this letter *in his hand* from me, because I want to tell him "Thank you so much"
And the letter said, 'I'm that nun, you won't remember, blaah blaaah.'
Well, he put it in his hand,

And he opened the card and he got really emotional
And he said
'My god, thoughout all these years I've always wondered what happened to that wee nun'

Well. I did alright.
Thank you, Billy!

Flump Sheep

Imagine no just meeting him, right,
Which is amazing.
Cause that's a story, meeting the Big Yin, eh?
Oh aye, straight up.
That's no nuhin' ye know.
That's no a normal day.
Sure there's loads eh folk where, if you met them, ye'd be like

Fuckin' . . . there . . . Ah dunno
Paolo Nuttini, right
And they're most likely no geein' a fuck
Right?
Ah mean, Ah actually like Paolo Nuttini
He's got a cracking voice
Ma ex couldny stand him
But that's no saying much.
Didny like Flumps.
Ye know what Ah mean
Who doesn'y like a Flump fuck sake
I'd be eatin' a bag eh Flumps
Good wans anaw,
None eh yer foam squishy no quite Flump hings
Or anyhin fae Spar or Poundland or that
Ah'm talkin' brand Flumps
And I'd go 'Want wan?'
And the face'd just go (*Wipes hand down face as changes to a gads look.*)
So what can ye do?
Ah mean you'd take a Flump if it was offered aye?
Aye, exactly, cause you're normal.
You'd need tae be aff yer nut tae say no tae a Flump, eh?
. . . or a diabetic.
But . . . even then you'd . . . Ah mean
What's wan Flump gonnae, you know what Ah mean?
Ach Ah don't know, maybe it wid.
Ma son's got diabetes
Ah'll need tae ask him
Right, well, it was good talkin' to you
You take care.
What?
Oh Christ aye, sorry, fuck, the Big Yin, aye!
So, aye, Ah'd be excited to meet Paolo Nuttini
Cause he's magic
Good kid
'Singin' the song and this is the life sanananananananananana
Jimmy's front door'

But I'm sure most folk'd just be lit that
'Oh aye, look there he is, there's that guy off the charts'
Or if you came home and you were like
'Ah met Paolo Nuttini the day'
They'd be lit
(*Shrugs.*) 'Cool'
or lit
'Ah don't like him'
Or something

But see right, if ye met the Big Yin, right?
You'd go home and no matter what folk were saying
You'd be like
'Shut up, whatever you're sayin's a load eh shite
Compared wi what Ah'm about tae say'

And then you'd tell them
And they'd be like 'Whoa that's amazing! What was he doin'?'
And here's the thing, he wouldn'y even have to be doin anyhin
Like anyhin mad or excitin' or that cause it's just amazing itself.
It's like if ye saw . . . a snow leopard
Folk wouldn'y ask you what it was doing
They'd just be like, 'Fuckin' hell, no way!'

Like, bein' next tae him like
Is enough,
Ye know
Just bein' in his presence,
Just that you were there
And he was there
Ah don't know
Sounds fuckin' stupit
But it would make you feel more alive
Or more yourself or something
You know
Cause like there he is

And I'm here,
Ah don't know
But point is folk'd be lit that
You know
Ye'd be pure made up.
Like in the persence eh greatness or what
But like also wan eh us, ye know
It's like
You'd be like God there he is
Then ye'd be like
Man, the Big Yin is *real*
And then ye'd be like
He's wan eh *us*
And he's *amazing*
So lit *we're* amazing
So like, in a way, *Ah'm* amazing
Ye know what I'm saying?

I bet you he'd take a Flump if ye offered him
Just sayin'

But like, aye, so just meetin' him's a story
But. Here, would it no just be magic to hang out wi him eh?
Imagine it.
No just meetin' him
But like hangin' out
No hangin' out
(Who the) fuck 'hangs out'
Well, ye know what Ah mean
Like going for a pint wi him like
Well, no a pint cause he doesn'y, ye know, hingy
And fair fucks tae him
Well, like, go for a coffee or what
But like no that cause that's
I hate goin, for coffee
Shite
Ah like coffee just don't want to go for wan
Look ah can have a pint and he can have a coffee
Or a Fanta or an Irn Bru or whatever

Point is it'd be mental
Just cuttin' about wi the Big Yin
Fuck a pint actually go up a hill wi him or somehin
Chase sheep about or
Like chuck hings intae the sea
Like rocks like
No a sheep or anyhin
Though if he telt me dae it
Ah'd dae fuckin' anyhin
Ah'd chuck a sheep in the sea if he telt me tae
Fuck, Ah'd chuck ma maw in the sea if he telt me
Or like just run about we ma willy out
Ye know
The way he does
Aye man, it'd be magic

Montage Three

1 *I'd Prob'ly Kiss His Feet*

They shoes are in the People's Palace.
You know they big banana shoes he wears?
They're in the People's Palace . . .
It's closed the day.

If I met him?
I'd prob'ly kiss his feet
I'd prob'ly kiss his big banana feet
If ah could ask him anyhin?
Eh
How you been, Billy?

2 *Scones*

He came to my house and he ate my scones. He was only meant to have one scone and stay for about half an hour. He stayed for two and a half hours, he had five scones, and he finished aw my jam. He said it was great jam, they were lovely scones and it was a lovely wee hoose. He said ye don't really see hooses like this anymore and that I should be really proud eh it. And I tell you what, see after that? I really wis.

I kept asking him questions, what he was up to and how he was doin' but he didn'y want that, he was just like who are *you*? What are *you* like? What makes *you* happy? And Ah tell ye whit, after aw this Ah felt, Ah felt. absolutely marvellous.

3 *Granny's Floor*

He slept on ma granny's floor . . . what is that no good enough for you?
Ach who the fuck's ever slept on your granny's floor?!

4 *Scotia Bar*

Ah'll tell you wan. Ah was in the Scotia Bar one time right, and I go to the bogs and it's just me and him. And he goes off into the wee place to do his . . . business, ye know. And then he leaves. And Ah'll be honest . . . Ah hung around for a wee minute just tae breathe it in!

5 *A Kind Bull*

He is a kind bull, that's all I'll say. That's all I'll say, he is a kind bull.
I'll say no more. I'll say no more –
my only claim to fame was that I pushed him in the pram when I was twelve
But I'll . . . I'll . . . I'll say no more than that, I'll say –
He's doing very well, he's keeping very well, everyone is –
I'll say no more. I can say no more.

6 *I Would Go Anywhere with that Man*

I would go anywhere with that man.
I would go to the Tory Party Conference with that man!

Nearly Met Him Once

I tell you, Ah nearly met him once.
And I'll tell you what Ah mean by that.
Ah was at the cinema one day, watching a film
It wis an old one, a Laurel and Hardy thing.
And the film's going on
And it's all good.
And then, my God, few rows in front eh me. Laughin' away, hair bobbin' about, slapping the thigh – Connolly!
And, well, the film goes out the windy at this point.
They could eh been playin' anything and I'm no even aware eh it
Could eh been a vidjo eh ma maw, back fae the deed, tellin me where she'd hid the money
No that we hud any
But it'd go *whistles* over ma head
Cause all I'm thinking is,

Right, how am I gonna 'accidentally' bump intae him and then become pals
Maybe head off after it thegither and get a wee ice cream or something like, ye know?
A wee banana split!
Ah canna wait, this'll be brilliant
Ah'm thinking maybe Ah should go to the toilet and come back and get the 'wrong seat' and then Ah'd be sittin' beside him
Like that . . .

But I decide that I'm going to time it so we're both getting out the row at the same time.
And Ah'll just act all casual. Talk about the film like Ah don't know who he is
Be like:
'Aw, wint that amazin', eh? They don't make them lit that anym . . . Oh here, hawd on. You're the Big Yin. How you doin? I'm Patrick.'
BAM! Friends for life.

So it comes to the moment.
Film's done.
Right, which way's he gonna go? Which way's he gonna go?
Left! Right, play it cool, play it cool.
His row's busier than mine so I'm taking ages wi ma coat and lookin' for stuff on the floor
So that I can get my timing just right, and I get it perfect. Ah get it bang on, I get right to the end of my row, just as he's passin'
But
Erm.
Aye, well, it was Susan Balfour fae three streets over.
She hadny done her rollers. Hair was huge. Fair play to her.
Ah've never told her that tae this day.
Maybe I shouldn'y eh used her name
But look, there you go, that's how ah nearly met Billy Connolly
Kind eh.

Pish Yer Pants Funny

Oh I tell you he is pish yer pants funny.
Literally.
Ma sister went tae see him, right,
and he was –
here this wee recorder box hingy cannae see ma face, can it?
No? Good. Alright.
Right, so she's there
and he's hilarious.
And she's loving it
but she's desperate for a . . . for a pish, you know?
And, aw listen, she tells it much better than me,
But, right, he's been going on for hours
And she's loving it, she's no wanting him tae stop
But she kinda is.
Because she's absolutely bursting for this pish
and she's no wanting tae miss a second eh it.

No a bit.
So she's thinking: 'Here I'd rather that the whole show just stopped noo so everybody missed oot', ye know?
So she's hawding it in
and hawding it in
and it's gettin harder and harder
cause he's gettin funnier and funnier
And he's tellin' this story
An it's buildin' up tae a right good laugh,
about geein' somb'dy a fright, ye know.
And the way he's tellin' it, ye know he's gonna have a big Hilarious punch line.
The whole room can feel it and he's got them aw ike that,
Palm eh the hand stuff
Lit a school class, aw listening and like they shouldny be laughing but they cannae help it
And he's building the story up and up
But then he keeps resetting it and starting again
and every time he does
the whole room's more and more in hysterics
(*He's*) Playing with them
Knows exactly what he's doin'
Genius
And the crowd are loving it.
But no Sandra.
Because she. Is. Strugglin'
And now, every time she laughs
She's letting out just . . .
just a wee bit ah pish.
So now she's panicking
thinking 'If he doesn'y finish soon, I'm gonna explode'
But then she's just like that
'Fuck it, ye only live once', right?
And so she decides, right, tae just let a wee bit out
Just a tiny wee bit,
Ye know, just to give her a wee . . . buffer, to work with, you know?
A wee safety margin.

So she does, right.
She lets oot a wee bit
And it's some relief
But here. She's just about tae pinch
Or whatever it is lassies do, right?
She's just about to
But it's like he knows, right
Like he's been working up tae this aw night
and BAM, right when she's at her most vulnerable,
He does it.
Brings the whole show to a close,
Everyone one's in bits
And so's she.
Cannae get it tae stop so she's just lit that
'Well, I'm away noo, why stop? Fuck it. I'm happy, I'd rather be here, hearin' this covered in ma ayn pish than on my todd peein' in the bogs while everyone else gets to enjoy this.' So aye, when I say pish yer pants funny, I really mean it!
I tell you what, it was freezin' that night,
Her legs must he been lit ice
Mind you if you think it was bad fur her, ah had tae pick her up.

Aunt Fanny

Oh, that man cost me ma teeth.
HAAAAAA
Cause listen, right, ma name is Fanny
Short for Fantastic, right, HAAAAA
Naw, it's just Fanny
Fanny wis quite a common name back then
Hardly any Fannys about these days
A lot eh fuds, mind you, eh? HAAAAA
but hardly any Fannys
Anyway, Ah loved bein' a Fanny
And I especially loved bein' an Aunty Fanny
Cause eh his song about Saltcoats

'A stick eh rock Fur My Aunty Fanny'
This wee fella sitting on the train,
He's had a miserable time at the fair in Saltcoats
But he's still remembered to get his wee stick eh rock for his Aunty Fanny
Noo, Ah've got four sisters and three brothers
And they've aw got enough weans between them tae run a factory
And tae aw eh them, I am their . . . Aunty Fanny
And so wherever they go in the world
They're always bringing me back a wee stick eh rock
And I love it
It's one of those nice wee things
Started years ago when my oldest sister took her kids tae Blackpool
Fur the first time
Came tae ma house when they got back and got the wean tae sing it when she handed it over
Cute as a button
That became a story and then it became a tradition
So Ah've had rock, or sweeties where you cannae get rock, fae aw ayer the world
And so Ah feel like, in a way, ah've seen the world, or had it brought to me
Cause I've not been past the Paisley Road, what wi ma two bad knees and ma humphy back
So I've Billy to thank for that
I'm well travelled. Ah'm well travelled wi sweeties
But
Yer right, ma teeth did *not* thank him for it, haaaaa
Wi the number eh weans there is noo, wi aw the nieces and nephews Ah've got,
And grandnieces and grandnephews
Ah'm drowning in sweeties there can be a stream eh sweets pourin' in fi the Ester break
When they start swannin' off, right through tae the October break
And then Christmas starts and it's, ach, whatever

Aye, so he's why Ah lost ma teeth
But not to worry
I've got wallopers in
Naw. No wallopers, my God. HAAA
Wallies. WALLIES. Wallopers, naw, that's, thats a big . . . (*Mimes a big penis.*) mind you I've hud a few eh them in ma mooth as well
But naw. HAAAAA

Willy Freedom

He's always goat his Willy oot.
Ye know?
Always jumping about geein it, 'Aw, here, are ma knob. Look at it!'
No lit that like. Naw. No like, ye know, wan eh they wrong ins, you know? No lit, 'Here, look at it.' Or 'Fuckin' touch it, or anyhin' lit that. Naw. Fuck.
Naw it's more lit. Freedom. Lit, liberatin. Lit, natural, ye know.
No I don't think he's dain' it tae . . . show off. Naw.

God ah widnae fancy he's chances if we was dayin it tae pull. He's kind he like a Johnny bag full eh custard. But in fairness that's just cause he's got a real body, ye know, and that's kind eh more lit what real bodies look like. No like these wans ye see on the telly. Aw lit that. Aw . . . You know. Aw . . . (*Does aren't I fancy gesture.*)
Ye know? Real. So when he's cutting about baw naked I feel alright cause I feel like Ah see masell up there ye know.

Swearing Funny

My parents found it funny
And there was swearing
They liked something with swearing in it!
Well that was a fuckin' eye opener

Joke about a Bottom

I remember my dad laughing his head off at a joke about a bottom
About how he parked a bike in a woman's bottom
I didn't really get it I just knew it was a grown-up joke

That Man Ruined My Life

That man ruined ma life. And Ah'll tell you how. Ye know that routine he does about what to do if you ever get caught, you know . . . (*Does masturbating gesture.*)
Well, I'll tell you it right noo, right, he says, 'If you get caught, just go lit that; oh thank fuck yer here! There was a spider and it went right up my leg and I had to shake it off really hard ye know what I mean?'
Right?
Well, I found this very funny. I did. For years. Aye, and it hung around the back eh ma head and I thought, 'That'll come in handy, no that'll ever get caught, that's no gonna happen.' Until it did!
Now I cannot explain to you the panic that comes through your body when that moment comes. And I'm trying to remember what he said to say. And I remember some of it which I commit to quickly but I forget the second half. Ye know, the bit about the spider. So when my mum opens my bedroom door and I'm panicking thinking, 'What was that thing, what was that thing?' And so all I say to my mum in that situation is:
'Thank fuck you're here!'

Not Allowed to Watch Parky

We wurnae ever allowed tae watch Parky
No, never
Ma dad said it wus full eh lawless types
And folk wi mare money than sense

That were on it.
Aye, Rod Hull and Gene Kelly,
Real dangerous types
Anyway, there was talk at school
That the Big Yin was gonna be on
And we were excited like
It was like having Scotland at the World Cup
Wan eh yer own up there
Representin'
And being fuckin' class at it
Ye know?
And folk are aw
Ye gonna get tae watch it?
I'm watchin' it aye
You no watching it
And I'm lit
No Ah'll no be watchin it
No if ma dad's got anythin' to do wi it
'I have told you, that programme is a gateway to bad hings'

But I'm in ma room
And I hear the TV on
And sure enough
My old man's sittin' there
And he's only bloody watching it
Now, I canna say anyhin;
Cause even though I now know he wants to watch it
If Ah go
'So *you* can watch it and ah cannae'
He'd fuckin' . . . he'd just switch it off
No questions
bam, gone
'I was merely looking for the football highlights'
So my only option is to try and no get caught watchin' it behind him
Need to be dead silent
Which isn't easy
When you're watching the Big Yin

Where's the Balance?

How come he cuts about ring naked aw o'er the wurld,
And everyone's lit that: 'Nae bother, on yersel, here a knighthood'
Right? But when a get ma knob oot, Ah got three month up the bar-L?
Telling me that's fair?!
Ok Ah hid previous
And it was in a Dobbies.
But honest tae fuck where's the balance there wi that?!

Gary *checks in again with whatever is written on the piece of card at the back.*

Billy Saved Ma Life

What does Billy Connolly mean to me?
Well, I can honestly say that I tried to commit suicide
And it just so happened that with sheer luck that
There was a Billy Connolly on the TV
And I started laughing at it
and that was the first time I'd had humour
In a lang time

And when that happened the wife went
'Well, that's showing signs of positivity' and
She started ordering Billy Connolly tapes and DVDs
And I started watching them again
and the more I watched them
The more Ah laughed
And the more I laughed the less thought about
Trying to commit Harry Carry

Listened when I was wee
Went off and joined the army
Billy came back into my life
And saved my life, basically

When Ah meet him
Oh awww ma heart was racing
I had everything planned out what Ah was gonna dae
when he came round the corner
But Ah couldn'y dae anyhin
I just sort eh like froze and . . .
Oh he's more than that to me, a rock star, to me noo like
I mean there's no many people you can turn room and say
Yeah well, you actually saved my life

No I never managed to say
A fair wanted to
Right
I did want to turn round and say
Hey Billy, you might no know this but you saved ma life
And that would have got his attention
But
Naw
Ah was a bit
At the time
A bit maybe
Ah just thought, 'Nah'

Elder Sausage Robber

Billy came up to film a documentary a few years ago
And he came over to the wee cottage in Ross-shire.

He wanted to hear the track 'Rain'
Because he'd been talking about the weather in Scotland in the documentary
And ironically we'd had lovely weather that week
so 'Rain' wasn't really appropiate in a way
But it was a lovely opportunity to meet Billy
because of course he's an icon across Scotland.
But it was lovely to meet the person,
the human being, um,
he's always come across as sort of very genuine on the screen

but in, uh, he was just so lovely to meet in person,
um, I'm sure other people have said this who've met Billy,
that you know, you feel very, he feels very, he feels like part
of your family.
You know, you feel very comfortable with him,
And that comes from him.
Ye know, he just feels like someone who's very comfortable
in his own surroundings.
He just came back to our wee cottage and sat with everybody
And he was there for quite a few hours
um but he was just content
and he just exudes this calm and it was like having an elder
with you.
Others might have said the same.
But it was like having an elder,
like an old pillar in the community.
With wisdom.
And commanded respect.
And he listened to what everybody had to say
and there was no ego about him.
Um You know, he'd join in with a few things and
we actually felt really sad when he had to go, it was like
saying goodbye to someone, was like saying goodbye to
someone you knew really well. And he sort of lingered at the
car and he sort of said 'Oh, I'd better be off' and you know, I
think we both had a lump in our throats actually because it
was a bit like saying goodbye to your, your dad or your
grandad and we thought we might not, well, we probably
won't see him again, ye know,
because . . .
It was a privilege to have that afternoon with him really.
Ummm. But it's . . .
the thing I remember most about him was –
he has this *luminous quality* that's the word I would use to
describe him.
Um I mean he was lovely but it's little things.
Everyone talks about his dress style.
When he was with use he wasn't in a particularly flamboyant

outfit, he was actually quite casually . . . comfortably dressed.
But he still looked,
he always has his own style, an elegance,
and I goes 'Billy, I love your shoes'
just a kind of classy-looking brogues but there was
something a wee bit different about them,
ye know?
And he said, 'oh . . .'
he just looked at me and smiled and said
'Vivienne Westwood!'
and then he said and then he said
'Well, it has to come out somewhere' (*Laughs.*)
just a little aside as he was getting in the car ye know.
And he's just so easy to talk to.
I mean I don't want to take up all your time because you'll
probably hear the same thing over again.

Well, I was just so, they were chatting as they were down the
water at the Cromarty firth there and he was just very,
just very relaxed,
he was chatting about music and comedy
and how . . . he'd like to do a bit more poetry
but how he wasn't like how he didn't have the confidence to
do it, ye know?

Like two old souls together in a way but then he suddenly
said
'Oh I did write this thing about sausages'
and then he started quoting this thing about sausages,
this lovely poem about sausages
and um . . . he's just . . . I don't know
I think that's just the mixture of him being someone that's
just himself and obviously extremely well known which
makes things difficult for him.

I mean you've, you've probably heard this story but he was
telling us about when he was in London years ago and he
just nipped out to get some milk early in the morning and of
course wherever he goes people know him don't they?

And he suddenly heard someone going
Pssssst
in the bushes
Have you heard this story?
No, it's just we were chatting and he was saying
'Oh, it can be tricky when everyone knows you when you're on the street'
he says
'I was once in London and I just nipped out to get my milk.
And this chshchshchsh in the bushes
and a voice is going "BILLY, BILLY!"
And he's going "Hello, yes?"
And this guy stepped out
and he opens up his jacket and he's got a shotgun in it and he says, 'D'ye want to come and watch a robbery?' Like an armed robbery! And he goes, 'Eh, eh, eh no thanks, pal, I'm away to get my breakfast' and he scuttles off. But it's almost as if they were saying it respectfully, ye know: 'Hey hey, come and watch us while we're doin' our work, doin', a . . . a robbery.'
It's just laughable.
It's just like everyone feels like they know him,
Right through to the robber.
Ha ha.

Montage Four

1 *Fifty Years*

Fifty year I've known that man. And I've never met him once.

2 *I Use His Patter Every Single Day*

He's changed the way I talk. He's changed the way I think. I use his patter every single day of my life. Honestly. Just this morning right, when ma kid was annoying me and he wouldn't eat his breakfast, Ah wis lit that: 'Yer just a little joooobby!'

3 *Ma Story*

It's a true story he's tellin'. Cause it's ma story. And he's been telling it my whole life. He makes me think of my future. Because he, more than anyone else, connects me to my past.

4 *He Changed the Culture*

He changed the culture. Absolutely. He did. He gave us permission to not only talk, to write, to perform as ourselves, but he allowed us to *think* as ourselves. *That's* what he did. He *gave* us that.

5 *Keep It Up*

He come into mat shop once and I thought, 'Oh my God I'm gonna have to tell him.' So I walked up to him and I said 'Billy, I'm so sorry but I need to tell you something, I've been nicking your jokes my entire life!'
And he just looked at me and said . . . 'Keep it up!'

A shift, **Gary** *stands on top of the banana chair.*

Imagine the Queue!

Did you see, but, all that the other week that was goin' on.
Wi her, like
And how everyone was, ye know, and . . . kind eh hing
And aye, aye, I get it, like, I do.
Like, I get them wanting to be a part of it like
Cause like, that's kind eh what it was, like, ye know, kind eh thing
Wanting to be a part of it.
It's all like
Ye know, folk looking like, like feeling like, like
Like they want to be a part of it
Rather than actual like full-blown grief

It's no like when yer actual maw
Or yer aunty
Or a cat or something

dies
Where it's difficult to like
Function
Like to actual do hings.
Cause like your, hingy, broken. Ain't ye?
Like when ma maw, and auntie, and cat died,
I was
I was broken
Mind you, they aw died at once
And that was, man, that was a lot
but anyway my point is
It was nice,
Like it was
When she (croaked it)
And folk wanted to
And it was sad
Ye know
And that was a lot of people in the queue
It was
I'm no saying it wasny

But honestly,
I'm no even kiddin
But like
See if he ever . . .
And I don't even want to
Ah can't even (think about it)
Just like, that's no ever gonna happen, right?
But just
If he
When he you know
My God
Can you imagine the queue
Could you actually even just imagine the queue if he
Him
Was to be
You know, aw . . . lying in state for folk tae come see him
The queue'd go fae here tae fuckin' . . .

Ah don't know . . . Poland?
And that'd be actual grief
Like actual full-blown heartache, man
Cause how do you go on in a world
Wi out the Big Yin?
I guess ye have tae
But
Fuck me it's a grim prospect eh
I'll be honest, see at first
See when you came up and asked to talk I thought
well, actually, at first I thought, 'Fuck's this daft cunt, he can bolt.'
Cause I thought you were lit radio or some survey prick
But like when you said you wanted to talk about the Big Yin
I thought 'Aw magic, maybe this guy isny a prick', no offence
But then I instantly went 'Aw naw' pure shat it
Thought, aw God, is something the matter,
I was ready to fall apart
I'm no ready for that
Don't think anyone is
So dinnae scare me lit that
and jist
Ooft
Ye know?
Aye but naw
Naw obviously like we know that day'll come
But like
Who's ready for that?
I tell ye, no one!

Gary *checks a piece of paper on a table at the back of the stage before returning to centre stage.*

Gary Three

It is clear that we have again returned to **Gary***'s personal story and he is picking up from where we left off in* **Gary One** *and* **Two**.

Talking to him was a strange and comforting experience.
Like, I know I'd never met him before but somehow I felt like I had.
I dunno if it was that he felt like a favourite uncle or something
because he was so humble and generous,
or because he looks you calmly and respectfully in the eye.
Or if it was just because I'd seen him on the telly so much
Through my whole life
Ye know, whether he knows it or not
Or likes it or not
Whether *we* like it or not
He's a part of who we are.

So it . . . somehow felt like we were just picking up from where we left off.
Ye know?
Here, I'm sure it felt exactly the same for him. HA!

But it was, it was a nice chat
He really made me feel at ease
Like he obviously knows it's a big hing for people
to chat tae him
but he knows
He's just a guy having a chat
And that's what he made it feel like.
Normal. Even though it wasn't. But it was, ye know?
I can't remember it all.
Between the coffee and everything else it was a bit of a blur
But I thought
'Right, I'm gonna do it. Ah'm gonna ask him.'
Ah said:
'Billy. I want to make a show about you.'

And cool as you like he said:

'Can you no wait till I'm deed?'

And Ah said

'Billy . . . I've not got two years'

This is left to hang in the air. The shock of it.

. . .

And . . . he laughed!

I got a laugh oot the Big Yin!
And that felt . . . unbelievable.

It was like . . . getting a high five from Jesus

It was . . . magic
A magic wee moment

Except . . . Ah didn'y say that.
Ah *thought* it!
And I nearly said it
But . . . ah shat myself

I didn't do the Billy thing.
I didn't take the risk
I didn't do it
Ah shat myself

I said:
'Oh . . . eh . . . aye . . . yeah . . . no . . . no worries. Thanks, man.
I thanked him for his time.
Genuinely. It was a lovely experience.
But I was crushed
And I left and I went to the park to have a sad sausage supper.

And then I thought

'Naw.
Naw I'm sorry but . . .
I can't wait,
I want you to know, I want you to know what you mean to all these people.
I want you to know while you're alive, all the ways, big and small, that you matter to all these lives.
I want you to have that.

I'm sorry, Billy, but I can't wait.
So . . . there you go.'

The band starts playing.

Gary *joins the band and they sing 'Everybody Knows That' by the Humblebums. As the song ends it feels like the show could absolutely end here. But . . .*

One More Thing

One more . . .

The band drops down.

Gary *picks up the card he's been checking all night. He takes it downstage with him to address the audience one last time. He is holding the card close to his chest so that the text can't be seen. The next text is delivered like the intro and the* **Gary One/Two** *text.*

I've got this pal.
Colin Bell, lovely guy, massive hands
He should've been on the rivets, man.
'Spanner Hands' they call him.
Beautiful big nice hugs as well, a lovely guy
He worked as a tech in Pitlochry theatre
Right
And Billy was on that night
And he was dead excited
Best view in the house, in the wings
And all night Billy's checking this piece of paper at the back of the stage
And Colin's thinking
'Brilliant. Ah'm gonna get his set list after this.'
It's at the back of the stage, on a table, under a glass top
So it doesn't get blown away or lost or whatever.
And he's thinking
'Easy. I'll be first on stage. And I'm gonna grab it. Get myself a wee family heirloom. Nae bother tae spanner hands, that!'

So, the show comes to an end and the crowd's goin' wild
Billy takes a boy and heads off.
And Colin's straight on to grab the piece of paper
But of course Billy gets an encore so he's coming back on
And so Colin's like that, 'Oh fuck!'
And gets straight back off.
So Billy does another ten minutes, crowd goes wild again.
Whoop whoop, well done, thank you, goodnight
Kindathing ye know?
Then it's curtain down and Billy heads off again
Colin *waits* to make sure it's definitely finished
Then he heads straight to the back of the stage
And he gets to the piece of paper
And it's *not* a set list at all
Ye know what it said on it?

This piece of paper he's been checkin' it all night
I hope to God this is true
All that's written on it is just *three* words . . .

Gary *turns the piece of card round to reveal what is written on it as he tells us what was written on Billy's paper. They are, of course, the same.*

'Say. Something. Funny.'

End.

Methuen Drama Modern Plays

include

Bola Agbaje
Edward Albee
Ayad Akhtar
Jean Anouilh
John Arden
Peter Barnes
Sebastian Barry
Clare Barron
Alistair Beaton
Brendan Behan
Edward Bond
William Boyd
Bertolt Brecht
Howard Brenton
Amelia Bullmore
Anthony Burgess
Leo Butler
Jim Cartwright
Lolita Chakrabarti
Caryl Churchill
Lucinda Coxon
Tim Crouch
Shelagh Delaney
Ishy Din
Claire Dowie
David Edgar
David Eldridge
Dario Fo
Michael Frayn
John Godber
James Graham
David Greig
John Guare
Lauren Gunderson
Peter Handke
David Harrower
Jonathan Harvey
Robert Holman
David Ireland
Sarah Kane
Barrie Keeffe
Jasmine Lee-Jones
Anders Lustgarten
Duncan Macmillan
David Mamet
Patrick Marber
Martin McDonagh
Arthur Miller
Alistair McDowall
Tom Murphy
Phyllis Nagy
Anthony Neilson
Peter Nichols
Ben Okri
Joe Orton
Vinay Patel
Joe Penhall
Luigi Pirandello
Stephen Poliakoff
Lucy Prebble
Peter Quilter
Mark Ravenhill
Philip Ridley
Willy Russell
Jackie Sibblies Drury
Sam Shepard
Martin Sherman
Chris Shinn
Wole Soyinka
Simon Stephens
Kae Tempest
Anne Washburn
Laura Wade
Theatre Workshop
Timberlake Wertenbaker
Roy Williams
Snoo Wilson
Frances Ya-Chu Cowhig
Benjamin Zephaniah